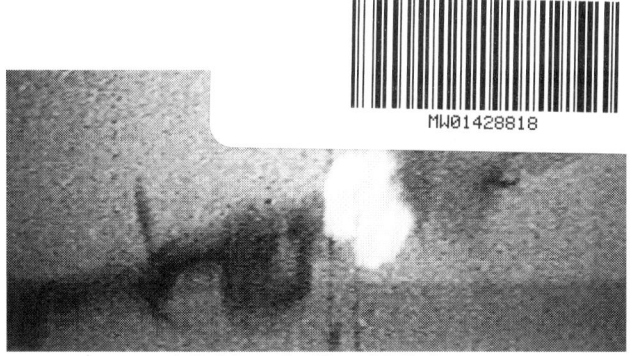

A B-24 on the Kassel Mission

2 Guys Talkin' B-24s
at a Cracker Barrel in Battle Creek, Mich.

April 12, 1999

Gene Crandall, Floyd Ogilvy
445th Bomb Group
Tibenham, England

an interview

By Aaron Elson

© 2013 Aaron Elson.
All rights reserved. No portion of more than 5 percent of this book may be reproduced without the written permission of the author.

Published by:
Chi Chi Press
(888-711-8265)

Other books by Aaron Elson
The Armored Fist: The 712th Tank Battalion in World War 2
A Mile in Their Shoes: Conversations With Veterans of World War 2
Nine Lives: An Oral History
Tanks for the Memories
Merry Christmas in July: B-26 Tail Gunner, ex-POW John Sweren
A Medic's Story

http://kasselmission.com
http://www.tankbooks.com
http://oralhistoryaudiobooks.blogspot.com

GENE CRANDALL AND FLOYD OGILVY

Preface

The Kassel Mission of Sept. 27, 1944, was one of the most spectacular aerial battles of World War II. Thirty-five B-24 Liberators that had flown off course, losing their fighter protection. Approximately 120 German fighter planes, Fokke-Wulf 190s and ME-109s. In a battle that lasted roughly six minutes, 25 B-24s were shot down, along with many of the German fighter planes, and one of the American P-51s that eventually joined the fight.

In 1991 a monument in Germany was dedicated to the memory of the battle, with the names of 118 Americans from the 445th Bomb Group and 19 Germans from four fighter squadrons who lost their lives that day.

When a German historian took me to the monument in 1998 and told me some of its history, I was hooked. Upon returning home, I discovered a posting by Tim Crandall in a B-24 forum in which he mentioned that his father was in the 445th. I contacted Tim, and he put me in touch with his dad, Gene Crandall, whom I arranged to meet during an interviewing trip in 1999. Gene brought along Floyd Ogilvy, a fellow veteran of the 445th. Ogilvy finished his required 30 missions in July and this was not on the Kassel Mission, and Crandall was a chief propeller specialist and all-around mechanical troubleshooter.

– **Aaron Elson**

The Kassel Mission Memorial in Friedlos, Germany

At a Cracker Barrel in Battle Creek, Mich.
April 12, 1999

Gene Crandall: My son wrote him a letter and said that his dad was always talking about Jimmy Stewart, and I was telling him what a great guy he was. He told Jimmy Stewart he really enjoyed "It's a Wonderful Life" and that his dad was always talking about him, so Jimmy Stewart sent me a letter. I didn't know him all that well. I talked to him about half a dozen times. [The actor Jimmy Stewart was an original squadron commander in the 445th Bomb Group, although by the time of the Kassel Mission he'd been promoted and transferred to a different group.]

Aaron Elson: You had mentioned on the phone that Stewart almost crashed.

GENE CRANDALL AND FLOYD OGILVY

Gene Crandall: Yes. It was at Sioux City. He was doing practice landings at night and there was a bad thunderstorm and he came in to land. He must have been a couple hundred feet high, and a bolt of lightning went right across the front of the canopy, and he lost it. He dropped it down and snapped off the nose gear, which was the weakest part of the landing equipment, and then the whole airplane went down the runway at like 45 degrees, and the sparks flew out from the landing gear strut, just like a dragging wheel. So I went out there with a couple other guys in a jeep, and Stewart got out of it and he was shaking and trembling, and all shook up, because he just damn near died. And the colonel was there. The colonel says, "You didn't see anything, did you?"

We said, "No, Sir, we didn't see a thing."

Aaron Elson: What kind of plane was it?

Gene Crandall: A B-24. We were in training at Sioux City, and then we went to Mitchell, South Dakota, to a satellite field after that. And from there we went to New York, Camp Shanks, and then we went over on the Queen Mary.

Aaron Elson: And you had mentioned an incident at Thanksgiving.

Gene Crandall: Oh, with Jimmy Stewart?

Aaron Elson: Yes.

Gene Crandall: Well, I went to, temporarily, before he got there – like you guys [Ogilvy] went through South America, and I went over to Cambridge, me and the chief inspector – they told us we were going to school. What we went over there and did was re-work these patrol airplanes that were looking for submarines. And they were all painted blue, they had sea waves on the bottom, and the engines, the sparkplugs hadn't been changed for 400 hours. That's a no-no. You should never, never let an airplane like that get more than a hundred hours, and the sparkplugs were snapping off right into the cylinder head, and we had to take little hacksaw blades and cut the shredded part out. Then we took a nail and put a wire around it with a battery and made a magnet and we reached out two sides of the cylinder and got the filings out. But anyhow, I was over there, and this airplane lands, and it's a B-24. This Ten-uv-us lands, it says T-e-n u-v u-s, and I says, "Damn, that must be some kind of a Latin name." And it struck me eventually that that was "Ten of us" in a crew. And that was Jimmy Stewart's airplane. And he got out, and I went over to it, and he looked at me and he said, "What the hell are you doing here?"

And I said, "We're over here, Sir, fixing these patrol bombers. They were using them for the submarines."

And he says, "You won't be here long." And within two hours, a 6-by-6 [truck] came and got us and we went back over to Tibenham. But see, he was awful sharp. He was a hell of a lot smarter than he appears in the movies. He was an architect.

Aaron Elson: I didn't know that.

Gene Crandall: Yeah, he graduated from college with an architecture degree, out of Yale.

Floyd Ogilvy: I think he graduated from Princeton, I'm not sure. [Stewart graduated from Princeton]

Gene Crandall: Well, anyhow, he said, "You won't be here long," and then we were sent back. And then on Thanksgiving, he came down to the mess hall and he was O.D., officer of the day, and he said, "Sergeant, can I sit with you?"

I said, "Yes, Sir." He was the squadron commander. And he sat down and he said, "How do you like the turkey?"

And I said, "Well, the outside's all right, but the inside's all frozen."

And he said, "Oh, my God." And then he got up and he went back, he found the mess captain drunk with a bunch of bottles around. They broke the mess sergeant down to private. Stewart didn't do that. And they broke the captain down to second lieutenant and put him on the China Clipper, you know, that dishwashing machine. And he had to stay on there for a whole month. So Jimmy Stewart wasn't exactly soft.

GENE CRANDALL AND FLOYD OGILVY

The last time I saw him, he'd been on one of those 12-hour missions, I thought he went to Berlin – [to Ogilvy] were they going to Berlin when you were there? I was checking him out when they hit the ground, because he was flying our airplane, a 700th [Squadron] airplane. I think he flew the 700th Squadron's airplanes because the Germans were after him. It would have been a great coup if they'd have shot down Jimmy Stewart.

Aaron Elson: So they knew about him?

Gene Crandall: Oh, hell yeah. The second day we were there Lord Haw Haw said, "Welcome 445th, Colonel Terrell.

Aaron Elson: He said that, really?

Gene Crandall: Yeah. Lord Haw Haw was the German propaganda man.

Aaron Elson: And did he mention Stewart by name?

Gene Crandall: No. But they knew about him.

Aaron Elson: Now, you being a ground crew chief, you were in the 700th Squadron?

Gene Crandall: Yes.

Aaron Elson: You were in charge of one plane?

Gene Crandall: No. I was the chief propeller specialist. I was also a B-24 specialist and I did troubleshooting on all airplanes, that kind of thing. Changed engines and propellers and all that. And hydraulics.

Aaron Elson: That must have been demanding, especially with all the damage.

GENE CRANDALL AND FLOYD OGILVY

Gene Crandall: Oh, it was very exciting. Hell, that was the greatest adventure of our life. You know, from 4 o'clock in the morning until ... well, it depends on the day. In the wintertime it used to get daylight at 9 o'clock in the morning, then it'd get dark at 4 o'clock in the afternoon. And then in the summertime it would get daylight about 4 or 5 o'clock in the morning, and it wouldn't get dark until 11 or 12 o'clock at night, because England's a long way north. Did you notice that?

Floyd Ogilvy: No, I didn't ...

Gene Crandall: That's so far north, it's almost as far north as Hudson Bay. That's a latitude or whatever it is that's way up there.

Aaron Elson: Did you work overnight?

Gene Crandall: Oh, yeah.

Aaron Elson: How did you work in the dark, with the blackouts?

Gene Crandall: Well, I've spent a lot of time in a goddamn blackout trying to put parts together that I couldn't see. One night I was working on an engine and we had a tent that went over the engines. And we got all pissed off, so we turned on a light. And we shouldn't have done that. A Spitfire buzzed us, and you could actually feel the breeze from that sonofagun, because that was a no-no. The Germans were always looking around there trying to find us. And we had anti-aircraft guns, but we never fired them, because we never wanted to give away where we were. If they came over, I don't know what kind of airplane it was, I think it was a diesel engine, they'd throttle back and they'd look and look and they'd drop real yellow flares. Their flares are real distinctly yellow and ours were real white, so we knew they were Germans. But they didn't bother us too much. The worst thing was the buzz bombs. Toward the end of the war they were shooting those buzz bombs one every couple of hours. And when the wind blew just right they'd go right over Tibenham, and then we'd all wait until we heard them go over. If they ever stopped we all hit the deck, because they'd be coming down someplace.

GENE CRANDALL AND FLOYD OGILVY

Aaron Elson: Did any of them explode nearby?

Gene Crandall: No.

Aaron Elson: Did you get attached to any particular plane or crew?

Gene Crandall: You tried not to, because these guys came and went at an ungodly rate. We lost, as I understand it, 150 bombers. And I got to really like a couple of guys, like one captain, I don't know what his name was, but he was a West Point graduate. He used to come down to the line all the time on his day off, and I used to give him lectures about flushing their propellers all the time because the damn oil congealed and the governors wouldn't work. Did you ever have that problem?

Floyd Ogilvy: Shoot, I was just a gunner. I didn't know what was going on.

Gene Crandall: But this guy was a wonderful guy. And of course, he got blown away. And that happened so many times, we just got to the point where we did our job and tried not to be buddy buddy with them. It was for self-protection. And even, one day I saw a picture of the body bags, and all that, that's 50 years later, I had all that crap down in my subconscious, and I woke up in the middle of the night screaming and yelling and thinking I was back in the damn war. And I'd never had a dream like that before. But that shows you how you, I'm sure that happened to you. Hasn't that happened to you?

Floyd Ogilvy: No. The thing that, most loud noises, I still remember the flak, because that was our major problem. Fighters we didn't have a problem with. Fortunately when I was there flak was the real problem. And when I go to a military funeral out here at Fort Custer and they shoot those guns off, I know they're gonna go, I still jump.

Aaron Elson: Describe the flak.

GENE CRANDALL AND FLOYD OGILVY

Floyd Ogilvy: Well, it came up in different ways. For example, we went to Berlin and they had what we called block flak, where I mean it was like a city block, the guns would all come up.

Aaron Elson: A city block?

Floyd Ogilvy: Yeah, it was a block, we called it block flak. They didn't track you. They knew your altitude. They knew you were gonna fly about 24,000 feet, and they would shoot those up. Of course I'd be chucking that chaff out, trying to screw up their radar. And so it was really a very frightening thing, and there was nothing you can do about it. That was our major problem.

Aaron Elson: Did you see planes to the left or right of you get hit?

Floyd Ogilvy: Yes. I had one off of my right wing, it was shot down over Belgium. It took a direct hit right behind the pilot's area, and it peeled off. My pilot said, "Check and see if there are any chutes." I checked. I didn't see any chutes. And as it went down, one of the wings came off, it looked like a leaf.

Gene Crandall: Did you ever see an airplane that was captured by the Germans and rebuilt?

Floyd Ogilvy: A B-24? I never had seen one but I heard they had them.

Gene Crandall: They used to, when they had crashes, they fixed them up and they'd get right up there in the same formation with our guys and radio down the altitude and the speed and all that, and then dive out of the formation and then you'd get the flak. Right?

Floyd Ogilvy: Well, yeah, I never saw one of those, but I knew. ... What is your interest in this?

GENE CRANDALL AND FLOYD OGILVY

Aaron Elson: I've written a couple of books about my father's tank battalion, and I was over in Europe, in Germany, doing some research, and I met Walter Hassenpflug.

Floyd Ogilvy: He was one of the people that got shot down?

Aaron Elson: No, he was a 12-year-old kid, German, and he captured Frank Bertram. He told me the story, showed me the monument, and I was hooked. I went to a reunion of my father's tank battalion after he passed away, and I'd hear these veterans telling stories, and I was just riveted. So I went back the next year with a tape recorder.

Gene Crandall: There's a lot more interest now in the Second World War, 50 years later.

Floyd Ogilvy: I just came back from Pennsylvania, Penn State University, they had the National Collegiate Wrestling Tournament there, and I'm an ex-college wrestler so my wife and I go every year.

Aaron Elson: Reg Miner was a wrestler in high school.

Floyd Ogilvy: I don't know that name. Is he 445th?

Aaron Elson: He was the pilot of Frank Bertram's plane. I think Kassel was his 19th mission. When did you finish your missions?

Floyd Ogilvy: August 11 and that was September 27 as I recall.

Aaron Elson: So he would have come in shortly before you finished up. What missions did you go on besides Berlin?

Floyd Ogilvy: Munich. Strasbourg. Saarbrucken.

Aaron Elson: Oh, Saarbrucken. I don't know if it was the same one, but his plane was badly damaged on a Saarbrucken raid and he landed in a field.

GENE CRANDALL AND FLOYD OGILVY

Floyd Ogilvy: In England?

Aaron Elson: Yes. But he didn't make it back to Tibenham. He came in over a clump of trees and they were scraping the bottom of the plane. It was just a miracle, but that was a Saarbrucken raid.

Floyd Ogilvy: There was more than one Saarbrucken mission. But I did go there once.

Aaron Elson: You were not on the Gotha raid?

Floyd Ogilvy: No, that was before I got over there.

Aaron Elson: But you had heard about that?

Floyd Ogilvy: Yep, I sure did. I was scared to pieces. That was a tough one.

Aaron Elson: Did you ever go to Gotha?

Floyd Ogilvy: No. It happened before I got there, where they lost several planes from the 445th.

Aaron Elson: Do you recall the plane that, when they sent four planes up to Ireland and they brought one back and the plane blew up in midair with the four crews on it?

Floyd Ovilvy: My navigator got killed in that. John Hennessy. In fact, it's in this book ["Fields of Little America," by Martin Bowman], it tells about it.

Gene Crandall: What were they going to Ireland for, to pick up another airplane?

Floyd Ogilvy: Yes. They had 24 guys on it, and the plane blew up. And my navigator, after I finished my tour, my navigator stayed in.

GENE CRANDALL AND FLOYD OGILVY

Gene Crandall: You know, after this raid that you were talking about, the Kassel mission, the next day we had 31 brand new airplanes. Because they had them in a staging area. And I thought to myself, thank God for the civilians that are building this stuff. And I guess Ford built them so fast that they had to slow him down because he was making one an hour. After I got through college I went to law school and so forth, I went broke, so I went over to Kaiser, they had Willow Run then, and I was a division superintendent building C-119 cargo airplanes in the same place that all those B-24s were built. And as far as I know about B-24s, any airplane built by Ford we could take the tail section off of any Ford plane and put it right on there and he built them all with pictures and everything so that they always were a perfect fit. But the Consolidated airplanes are lousy, they were almost hand made in a different way.

Aaron Elson: So both Ford and Consolidated made B-24s?

Gene Crandall: Oh, a lot more than that made them. I don't know how many plants made them. I think they made them, didn't they make B-24s in Texas?

Floyd Ogilvy: In Oklahoma.

Gene Crandall: In Oklahoma? Consolidated, I don't know if they built them in Wichita or not. They had an awful lot of components being built and shipping to the assembly place. But I know they slowed Ford down because they were making one an hour, and boy, I think the civilians did as much to win the war as we did. Because one time we had a bunch of construction guys screwing around with our runway and they spilled crushed rock all over the ground, were you there then?

Floyd Ogilvy: Uh-huh.

Gene Crandall: We had to ground all our airplanes because they were running over these damn crushed rocks. And within 36 hours, airplanes were arriving with loads of tires. And the people in the United States were really getting it together. I guess we could thank Marshall for that. Marshall was the brain behind the whole damn war.

Aaron Elson: Did you encounter any signs of sabotage on any of the planes?

Gene Crandall: No, I never saw any signs of sabotage. I know that one day a little black car pulled up and snapped up about three Englishmen that were working on the runway. I don't know what exactly they were, but it was the CID, and they had spies there, I know that. Because they knew when we were taking off and every other damn thing. But this little black car came up there and plainclothes guys got out and snapped a couple of these Limeys off of the runway and took them away. But I told you, two days after we got there Lord Haw Haw said "Welcome to the 445th." They had spies, but I never saw any sabotage. We had enough wrecks due to our own stupidity. I was much more frightened by our own people than I was the Germans, because we had some gunnery officer that was trying to sight in the rear turret and he didn't have the interruptor on, the fire interruptor, and he was spraying bullets all over the base. In fact, I went over to my washerwoman one day, she used to wash my clothes, and I went over there and she says, "Come along in here now," and I went in there, and she had holes in her parlor. And I said, "My god, where's that from?"

She said it was from those machine guns.

The worst problem we had, because I used to go down there in the dark, in the morning, and the armament guys would be fiddling around with the turret, and every once in a while a blast with those incendiary bullets would go right out over the base, because the guys hit that foot pedal you guys had in there.

Floyd Ogilvy: They had them in the tail turret, a manual thing to fire the guns in case the hydraulic system or something was out. I can remember, in one of the bases where I was located, I'm not really sure where it was, but a guy got in the back in the turret while he was on the ground and stepped in the turret and hit that, and it sprayed bullets all over the place.

GENE CRANDALL AND FLOYD OGILVY

Gene Crandall: Yeah, and I was riding down the perimeter, dragging a propeller, or an engine, I forget which one I was dragging in a jeep, and that guy was still practicing over there and the damn bullets hit the trailer, or the dolly that was hauling the engine. I was with a guy, and we heard that pinging going on. I said, "For Christ sakes, stop!" And we jumped out of there, we looked, and there was a hole in that damn, well, those were armor piercing bullets. I walked by a turret one time, a tail turret, and I told the armament guy, the guy who took care of the machine guns, I said, "There's a jammed cartridge in that gun. Now be careful." I walk by the gun, and this guy got in there, and it went off. And it just missed the back of my head. It hit the ground, ricocheted right through an engine, and out through the wing. And I couldn't hear for a week. So my assistant, I said to him, and this guy had his fingers, you know, where the air cool slots are, in a .50-caliber, he had his fingers in there, and they nipped off the end of his fingers, and he came out of there screaming and we grabbed him and put him in a jeep and took him over to the hospital. But those old bombers were very, very dangerous. I don't know how many of them had gas leaks, and if a B-24 ever cracked up it rolled up. Very few of them stayed whole when they came to rest, did they? The 17 was a good, tough airplane to crack up in.

Floyd Ogilvy: We don't talk about 17s. We're 24 people.

Gene Crandall: Some 17 pilots used to come over to our base and they'd look at our engines, and our engines were real clean ...

Floyd Ogilvy: Because the 17s were Wright engines and ours were Pratt-Whitney and they ...

Gene Crandall: The Wright engine had a lousy seal where the front bearing is, you know, where the propeller shaft is. And they were always dirty, and the pilots would come over there and they'd say, "How do you keep that propeller clean?"

Floyd Ogilvy: You didn't have to. Did you ever hear of a guy by the name of Tony Marks?

GENE CRANDALL AND FLOYD OGILVY

Aaron Elson: No.

Floyd Ogilvy: He's a guy that I have been in touch with, and the plane that we flew most of our missions on was called the Silver Streak, and I didn't realize that it had been shot down before we left, and we flew our last four missions on a plane called Thumper. So I got hold of him and I told him, no, I said my plane was, I thought it got shot down on the Kassel raid. He wrote me back this letter and he said ...

Aaron Elson: (reading) "Dear Floyd, Nice to hear from you. Again I thank you for the confirmation of my info re the Silver Streak. Memory is a funny thing and you're not the first vet by any means to tell me something which conflicted with the facts that I had. When you do this type of research, you just have to have an open mind about things and not be too dogmatic. It's odd, though, that Birsic's book ["The History of the 445th Bomb Group," by Rudolph Birsic, who was the group adjutant] records no losses on July 25 whereas [Roger] Freeman's "Mighty Eighth War Diary" does, just one 445th. I'm familiar with the other plane you mention, Thumper ..."

Floyd Ogilvy: My plane got shot down on July 25, and then we flew on the Thumper and he talks about that there, too.

Aaron Elson: (reading) "...In fact, I have a couple of photos of it, one with the nose turret knocked off after a midair collision during a mission to Mainz on 9 September '44. After you finished your tour, I should think. Thumper was finally lost on a mission to Hanau on 11 December '44." Oh, he's in England, this ...

Floyd Ogilvy: Yeah, he's an English person, and he was just really very interested in ...

Gene Crandall: You were in the Normandy invasion?

Floyd Ogilvy: Yes. I flew two missions on D-Day.

GENE CRANDALL AND FLOYD OGILVY

Gene Crandall: I think the group flew three missions that day. Because I know we put up everything we had, even War Weary airplanes, with a big WW on the tail. War Weary, did you ever see them?

Floyd Ogilvy: No.

Gene Crandall: When they get all worn out they put WW on the tail, they call it War Weary. And they sent everything they could get up. And one of these planes came back with the propeller not feathering, just turning, and I went over and grabbed hold of the blade, twisted it, and the damn thing went back and forth six inches. Somehow the hydraulic reservoir got shot out of there, and that airplane was in such bad shape that if anybody flew in that plane they were taking their life in their own hands. Well hell, they just junked them all, didn't they? Like when I was down to Ipswich [an RAF landing field at Manston] where this one airplane came in that we picked up, I was telling him there was a runway five miles long, and one mile was blacktop and the rest of it was gravel, and they had pipes all the way down each side of that runway where they'd dump gasoline, and then start it on fire, and then that would dissipate the fog. There was a lot of night work going on from the RAF. And the reason they did that was to dissipate the fog and then those guys knew where the runway was. And they had, it seemed to me hundreds of airplanes there, night fighters, all black, painted jet black. And they had all kinds of British airplanes there, and they were all piled up. It must have been billions of dollars worth of airplanes. Ipswich is right on the coast, so they'd come out of Germany and that's what they hit. But they had an interesting system. When these guys would come back at night, they'd have one searchlight. When they got to the coast, the British had this searchlight system, and they'd have one searchlight right up and you could see that thing from 10,000 feet. And then the guy would fly to that searchlight, and they'd turn it off, and they'd light another one down there about ten miles, and he'd fly to that one. And then when they were through, they could tell by the sound of the engine where it was, when he got down there far enough, why they'd let him land. Well, one morning I went down to the line and there were about twenty of those great big Halifax bombers sitting there that had gotten weathered in at their own base and they landed at our base, because they flew at night. And we used to listen to them at night going over, you could hear them at night, one right after the other.

These guys flew every day, all day long, in formation. At the end of the war there were thousand plane formations, and when they're flying up there you could see, you remember when they were all aluminum? They stopped camouflaging them because they'd go seven miles an hour faster if they were aluminum. So these parts would come trickling down like chaff, like you were talking about like Christmas tree chaff, and you could see it come down from 15, 20,000 feet. Very interesting time.

Aaron Elson: What was the mood on the base on Sept. 27, after the Kassel raid?

Gene Crandall: We took it as a terrible, terrible loss. I mean, when you lose 31 airplanes, you know, everybody said, "Oh my God." Well, there was a time, you know, when they almost stopped the daytime bombings, the losses were so terrible. But in that raid you're talking about, we heard that the German Goering's Yellow Nose Squadron jumped the whole formation. That was an awful sad day, Jesus, you lose 310 men, we thought we lost that many all in one crack [about half of the personnel in the crews of the 25 planes became prisoners of war. While only four planes actually returned to Tibenham, the other six either reached Manston or crash-landed in Allied territory with their crews largely intact]. That's why we didn't get to be too friendly with guys like this [Ogilvy]. And at the end of the war, as we grew older and the crews grew younger, they were like little kids. It was a lot of, like, almost like cannon fodder.

Aaron Elson: You must have had buddies who were crew chiefs of planes, how did they take it when their plane ...

Gene Crandall: Oh, they'd get sick when they'd lose their plane, because it's like part of them, a lot of crew chiefs went on missions with them.

Aaron Elson: Really?

GENE CRANDALL AND FLOYD OGILVY

Gene Crandall: Yeah, they did. I know half a dozen guys went on missions. I've been on missions. But they were milk runs. Never go along to Berlin. But hell, the crew chief got to be very close to the people, his crew. One crew bought a silver B-24 carved by a jeweler and gave it to the crew chief. And when they went to London they always brought him back a bottle of booze. The pilots were very nice to the ground crew, because their life was hanging on everything.

Aaron Elson: I can't get over, you know, reading the amount of damage to some of those planes...

Gene Crandall: Oh, gosh, you don't know. They'd come back with half a tail gone, and wings all shot to hell. In fact, one time one came back and he had a .20-millimeter right through the propeller blades, and we learned in engineering school if that ever happened it would really throw it off balance. I said to the pilot, "Did you know you had a bullet through the propeller?" He said, "Hell, no." He said, "I was so interested in getting back it didn't bother me."

Well hell, I don't know how many times they'd get shot on the deck, you know, down low, and the Germans would be after them and they'd call for 60 inches of manifold pressure and come back out of there and burn up their engines almost, and we'd have to change the engines. Hell, I've seen them come back and they actually sucked the duct business out of the intake manifold, and I'd say to them, "Jesus, you know you burned the engines out?" And they'd say, "We don't give a damn ..."

Well, they were sitting ducks, that's why they got down on the lower level, just to get back across that damn Channel. That Zuider Zee has still got thousands of airplanes, and they still dig 'em out of there once in a while, and that water's so cold that they find the guys' dog tags and all that. Which is right where the windmills and all that is.

Floyd Ogilvy: Was [Bill] Dewey a POW?

Aaron Elson: No, Dewey made it back to Manston. And, let's see, I think that was only his eighth mission, so he continued to fly. What led Hennessy to stay in?

GENE CRANDALL AND FLOYD OGILVY

Floyd Ogilvy: I don't know, if it was a promotion or what. Anyway, he stayed over there and I came back home, and I didn't know until way after the war that he was killed. A handsome young guy. Nice kid.

Gene Crandall: He got killed?

Floyd Ogilvy: Yeah, he got killed in that thing that he was talking about, those 24 people, they were going to Ireland.

Aaron Elson: They were delivering three old B-24s ...

Gene Crandall: Then they picked up new airplanes, didn't they?

Aaron Elson: No, the fourth plane went with them and brought the crews back. I guess there were six man crews on each. And over Liverpool it just exploded in midair. This fellow George Noorigian, he was a bombardier, he said it was his theory, nobody ever knew exactly what happened, but with 24 people on a plane he thought a lot of them would be smoking, and he thought there must have been a gas leak.

Gene Crandall: Well, the way the wind blew through there I don't know if that would have made any difference. Boy, if that wind blew through there it was cold. I've seen, the B-24 was notorious for leaking. I've seen guys when the plane would spring a leak, they'd get so damn mad they'd get out there and kick the airplane. We had some crazy fellows. One guy used to come back from a mission, and he'd have the co-pilot fly, and he'd get down there about ten feet off of the English Channel and take his .45 and shoot it down into the water. Well, wartime pilots are a little crazy. Especially fighter pilots. One guy was from Clear Point, North Carolina, and he owned a tavern or what they call a roadhouse, and he knew this guy that was either the first or second ace in the British Isles. So the guy came over there, and he's flying a jug, you know, a Thunderbolt, a P-37, and he said, "Show us a little performance, will you?" And this young kid, he was nuts, he was maybe 25, he looked like he was 30. And he took that damn jug aloft

GENE CRANDALL AND FLOYD OGILVY

and he made a pass at that field upside down, and you'd swear that that canopy was gonna drag the ground.

Aaron Elson: You had mentioned governors earlier. Did the engines have governors?

Gene Crandall: Sure as hell did. Hydraulic governors.

Aaron Elson: Was that to control the speed or to limit it?

Gene Crandall: To control the blade angle of the propeller. When you got up to 2,850 RPM if it ever got that high, the blade angle would take a bigger bite of the air so that the engine wouldn't run right, and if it got up to 3,500 it would burn the engine up.

Aaron Elson: Let me ask you, one of the pilots on the Kassel Mission who made it to the emergency field at Manston said that he had an almost panoramic view because he was in the lower left element, I think, but he could look out and see all that was going on, and he said one memory that would always stay with him, one of the weirdest things he'd ever seen, two B-24s, he said their propellers, all four propellers corkscrewed away from the plane and flew in formation until they tilted downward.

Gene Crandall: I've never heard of anything like that. I used to put propellers and engines on there, and it was my job to run 'em up to full 60 inches of manifold pressure, and the damn propellers were turning right by my head, and it was my job to run 'em up and check 'em out, and I never saw a propeller leave an airplane. But if he said he saw it he saw it. But it must have been some kind of engineering fluke.

Floyd Ogilvy: That was on the Kassel raid?

Aaron Elson: Yes. He felt that it was an inexperienced pilot in both planes that had given it full throttle, now I don't quite understand ...

Gene Crandall: That wouldn't make sense.

21

GENE CRANDALL AND FLOYD OGILVY

Floyd Ogilvy: It would if they feathered something and shouldn't have.

Gene Crandall: If they feathered it, that still wouldn't make them break loose.

Aaron Elson: Is it possible that it was at the same time as they were being hit by shells?

Gene Crandall: Well, to do that, you'd probably have to take the whole nose section off the airplane, and that nose section is made out of magnesium so it's lighter. But I never saw that happen. I saw one airplane once that had a rebuilt engine on it so that a nose section came off it, but I never saw. ... We had the best airplanes they could build, the best they could give us. I never saw anything like that.

Floyd Ogilvy: Well, anything is possible.

Gene Crandall: Well, in wartime, you know, they, like Ford built one an hour. If there was a defect it's possible. But I never saw anything like that. ... Where are you from?

Aaron Elson: New Jersey.

Gene Crandall: What part of New Jersey?

Aaron Elson: Hackensack, northern New Jersey.

Gene Crandall: I was in Trenton for a while. Fort Dix there. Till we got redeployed. I liked Trenton. George Washington slept there.

Aaron Elson: Now you became a lawyer after the war?

Gene Crandall: No, I went to law school. Oh, hell, I can't stand lawyers. I went broke in law school.

GENE CRANDALL AND FLOYD OGILVY

Aaron Elson: How did you do that?

Gene Crandall: Oh, I had a bunch of kids. Then I decided I didn't like lawyers anyhow. So I went to work at Kaiser. And 18 months later they were in a big aircraft program and I went over there and ended up a division superintendent building airplanes.

Floyd Ogilvy: Guys, I've got to get home, it's 9:30. It was nice talking with you.

Aaron Elson: Let me just get the name of this, "Fields of Little America, Martin W. Bowman."

Gene Crandall: Where did you get that?

Floyd Ogilvy: I bought it in England when I went over, after I retired. Saw it on the shelf and said, ooh, that looks interesting.

Gene Crandall: He's the mayor of Battle Creek.

Floyd Ogilvy: Not anymore.

Aaron Elson: How long were you the mayor?

Floyd Ogilvy: Three years.

* * *

Aaron Elson: There really is tremendous interest in the war.

Gene Crandall: I suppose this "Saving Private Ryan" really. ... But you know, I watch a lot of these periodicals and things, newsreels and all that, and I've learned more about the Second World War, what I was telling you about bombing Switzerland...

Aaron Elson: Oh, yes. Tell me again.

GENE CRANDALL AND FLOYD OGILVY

Gene Crandall: Well, you know this never has come to light, and I knew we bombed Switzerland. But until the Swiss got accused of hoarding the gold for the Germans and even the gold teeth out of the Holocaust victims, I never heard this until about three months ago, and they finally admitted it. But one day I was talking to these guys and I said, "Where are you going?"

And they said, "We're going to go to Switzerland."

And I said, "You can't bomb Switzerland, they're neutral." But they came back again, and I said, "Well, where'd you go?"

And they said, "We went over and bombed Switzerland."

I said, "What the hell did you do that for?"

And they said, "Because they were making ball bearings," and I heard that it was seven miles inside the border. They bombed the hell out of it. And then we apologized to the Swiss and gave them seven million dollars for destroying the building. But this same guy told me one day, he said, "I've got 24 missions." And he's from up here, not too far, I won't tell you. And he said, "I'll see you after the war."

And I said, "What do you mean you'll see me after the war?"

And he said, "Well, we've got 24 missions in and we've got to fly 25, so we're gonna abort when we get close to Switzerland."

And I said, "That's a hell of a note."

And he said, "Oh no, because if we go back we'll have to go to the South Pacific."

So he never came back. They aborted and went to Switzerland. And I saw newsreels, film, of about 30 bombers over there in Switzerland. And the Swiss were very upset that the Americans were over there. But this guy told me, boy, he says, "They've got a lot of beautiful women over there, and a lot of booze." And he says, "Since we put in our 25 missions, by god, we're gonna enjoy the rest of the war."

Aaron Elson: I'll be darned.

Gene Crandall: You didn't never know about that?

Aaron Elson: John Robinson in his book "A Reason to Live," have you read that?

GENE CRANDALL AND FLOYD OGILVY

Gene Crandall: No.

Aaron Elson: He was one of the originals, he went over, he kept a diary.

Gene Crandall: Did they know he kept a diary?

Aaron Elson: I don't know if they knew, but he kept it and when he retired he went back to it and he wrote just a day by day account, what type of bombs he carried, the things that he witnessed, you couldn't dispute. And he said one day that there was a bombing mission near Switzerland, and he saw two perfectly good B-24s peel off and head to Switzerland.

Gene Crandall: You know, at one time, the generals were very upset that they were aborting so much into Switzerland, and into Sweden, and they were gonna court-martial and so forth. But if they aborted and went to Switzerland and they had 25 missions, and boy, let me tell you, those missions were stacked up so they had 100 percent chance of getting killed, you sometimes wonder if they were smart to do it.

Aaron Elson: How can you blame them?

Gene Crandall: Well, I guess a B-24 cost about a half-million in those days. But if they put in 25 missions they had a hundred percent chance of getting killed, like this guy [Floyd Ogilvy] put in 30, he had a hundred percent chance of getting killed. He's a pretty nice old guy. He's getting old. I met him about 20 years ago one time down at an Irish pub. He's aged quite a bit since then.

Aaron Elson: How old are you now?

Gene Crandall: Seventy-seven. Oh, yeah, in fact I'm gonna start another business selling air purifiers.

Aaron Elson: How many children do you have?

GENE CRANDALL AND FLOYD OGILVY

Gene Crandall: Four. Well, I've got four and I've got an adopted daughter, I've got five, really. And you talked to Tim. He's a preacher.

Aaron Elson: Oh, is he?

Gene Crandall: Yeah. He and I totally disagree on that, you know, because I think it's a con artist, there's so many damn preachers taking people's money, I've always been dead against that. But he's got a black belt in karate.

Aaron Elson: Really.

Gene Crandall: Yeah, he was in the military, too. He asked me to be sure and tell him when you came here, but I called him twice and he's got, you know, when you call in and you get that bebop from the computer.

* * *

Gene Crandall: I think the 445th got three presidential unit citations, is that right?

Aaron Elson: I don't know.

Gene Crandall: Because they gave me one one time with a couple of stars. And I've got so many battle stars, the Ardennes and Europe, and I was just in a ground crew. About the only flying I did was test flying.

Aaron Elson: But did you get credit if your planes took part in those?

Gene Crandall: Oh, yeah. You're part of the group. That's how come I got these battle stars. We were only there for about 19 or 20 months, but I was with the outfit from the time it was organized in Wendover.

Aaron Elson: Do you remember the bomb dump explosion?

GENE CRANDALL AND FLOYD OGILVY

Gene Crandall: Oh, hell yes.

Aaron Elson: What happened then?

Gene Crandall: The bomb dump, there's another base, about, I don't know, it must have been three, four miles away, maybe five miles. And they had these super sensitive British bombs that didn't need a fuse. They'd just go off, and they were big. And these guys, now this is what I heard, I wasn't there, these bombs, they kicked them off a ramp and they had 6-by-6s with those V-figure that they load bombs in on with a hoist. And they kicked these bombs off, and I heard there were ten or twelve trucks there, and all the bombs went off. And the damn bombs went off for three days.

Aaron Elson: Three days?

Gene Crandall: Yes. As they blow up, then it would heat up the next, and go on and on. And it ruined all the airplanes on the base, because we went over and got the parts off them.

Aaron Elson: It ruined the planes on the base?

Gene Crandall: Oh, yeah. Because the blast ruined the tail sections and all, blew them apart, see. Yeah, that thing went off for three days. And our base had like five acres of bombs, and they were like six feet high. Boy, the civilians really kept us supplied. I think the civilians won the war.

Aaron Elson: Five acres of bombs?

Gene Crandall: Well, boy, that's a big operation. And the bombs all came in wooden boxes, then they'd stack them up. Well, we dropped, man, we flew 350 missions. Three hundred and fifty times about 20 airplanes, that's a lot of, nowadays they don't call them missions ...

Aaron Elson: Sorties.

GENE CRANDALL AND FLOYD OGILVY

Gene Crandall: Sorties, yeah. That's each airplane. But the B-24 was a very dangerous airplane. Not only did it leak gas to beat hell, it wasn't constructed in such a way that you could crash land it with any success. In fact, one time, three airplanes, when LeMay took over and they were flying close formation, and three of them collided right over my head. The two B-24s just came apart, disintegrated. And a 17 came over and the tail was cut off, and it went into the woods right by the base there. And then a lady that lived in the woods went over to try to help them and it blew up and killed her. We took up a collection for her children. But damn, I was standing there and watching and seeing all this orange-black fire, and I'm thinking, "My God, this can't be real." And then the parts started flying, dropping. But we had a lot of wrecks around our base. In fact, one time I was working on a pathfinder. I was working right off the end of the runway to a parking stand, and this is the time when the Bulge was going on and they needed air support desperately. And I'm working on this airplane and I'd just changed the governor and ran it up, and I got out of it, and our line chief came up. He was an old military guy, the only time you ever saw him, they said he was a drunk, but he's my drunken angel if you will, and he said, "Crandall, get the hell in this weapons carrier."

And I jumped in there and threw the bike in the back, because I had a bike, I had to, to go from airplane to airplane with. And we took off down the perimeter, and one came – this was when they were taking off in a dead fog – one came right out of the fog and clobbered the one I'd just been at, and the damn explosion hit us in the back, and it felt like our kidneys were floating. So we lost twenty guys right there. We lost a lot of airplanes. We lost about 150 bombers.

Aaron Elson: What was the pathfinder?

Gene Crandall: A pathfinder is a radar ship. When they first had radar, they could discern from the radar some things, and a pathfinder had a radar they could look down and see, like through the fog and so forth, and see cities and all. They had about two or three pathfinders to every mission, and the best navigators and the best bombardiers flew in the pathfinder. And at the end of the war, the pathfinders, they would all clue in on this pathfinder, and he had a tail light, and as he would signal, they'd drop bombs. And that's usually a major or colonel or something that was the navigator or the guy who was controlling, as they got better and better. I've seen pictures of bombardments where they're trying to hit a bridge and they dropped 200 goddamn bombs and never hit the bridge. You know, these new smart bombs are pretty neat. Boy, they dropped a lot of bombs over in Germany. They used to say, they used to come back across the English Channel and salvo their bombs, and they said you should be able to walk across the damn English Channel with all the bombs that are in there. Because they couldn't land with their bombs.

That was a very thrilling time. Not only that, it was great teamwork. Jesus, you had 5,000 guys in a bomb group.

Aaron Elson: What an experience that must be.

Gene Crandall: Well, it was the greatest thing that ever happened to me. I went to college, and I started a business, and I had a hell of an exciting life, and got a couple of divorces, the whole thing.

Aaron Elson: What had you done before?

Gene Crandall: I grew up in Pontiac, and I ended up working in Detroit making anti-aircraft guns, just before the war, and that's where I got a background in gears and all that crap. And I tried to get in the Navy as a pilot. I passed everything, but every time they'd check me, my pulse was too great. So then I went in the military over here, and they gave me tests for two days, the next thing I know I'm in Biloxi, Mississippi, and it says "Through these portals pass the finest airmen in the world." They never told you anything during the war. Then I went through the B-24 school. That, and we had the same training pilots did, like 4 o'clock in the morning through obstacle courses and all that crap. Then they had to eventually stop that because too many guys were having a nervous breakdown. And then they sent me over to Illinois, what's the name of that, Champaign, Illinois, and sent me to advanced specialist school, where I got engines and propellers and all that.

Aaron Elson: And you enlisted or were you drafted?

GENE CRANDALL AND FLOYD OGILVY

Gene Crandall: I enlisted in the Navy, and they turned me down because I'd get too excited, and then they drafted me. And my wife's uncle was the head of the draft board. He wanted to be sure nobody thought he was partial. He was a judge. But I learned more in the Air Force than I ever learned in my life. Well, you know, when you're in a combat outfit, for instance, these pilots used to want to abort an airplane, or ruin it. So they'd start the starter, and you had to nurse the starter, it'd go "rrrrrrrr," so they'd start the starter and get it up to speed, and then they'd mesh it, push a button, so they'd take their hand off the starter, and then they'd remix it again. And the second time they did it tore all the dogs out. So they'd say, "Well, we don't have to go today," because the airplane won't fly. So these guys, we got a big long spun G cord, I don't know if you know what that is, but it's a big long rubber cord, and we got leather and we made a pocket and we put it around the propeller and we took this damn 50-foot spun G cord and put it on the back of a jeep, put the top up on the jeep so when we pulled it and the damn thing let go, it wouldn't hit us in the head. Then they drove off sideways to the airplane and boy, when that spun G cord got stretched out there about 100 feet, and then kicked that engine, boy, that started. These guys invented it. And the crew chief, or the flight chief, would get in there and set the controls, so nobody could say the damn thing wouldn't run. And by god, we'd get 'em up there.

Aaron Elson: Now you mentioned the term dogs...

Gene Crandall: Dogs, they're catch gears. In other words, they fit in a slot and so forth, and when the clutch is engaged they grab hold of another gear and turn the engine, see. Oh, those guys invented a lot of stuff. See, these were a bunch of farmboys, or guys, like I grew up pretty much out in the country but not really on a farm, but, yeah, before I did, I worked on a farm too. Mostly we were just boys out of the Depression, and when I went to college, the professors in college said there'll never be another group like the guys in the Second World War, and I said, "Aw, you're crazy. Hell, there are good men all over."

They said, "Yeah, but just think about it. These guys grew up in the Depression. If they didn't work, they didn't eat. And they knew when they went to war they may never come back." Like I sold everything I owned when I went to war.

Aaron Elson: Really?

Gene Crandall: Oh, hell yeah. I was sure I was gonna get killed. Actually, when I went in was when Rommel chased the American army 120 miles through that Kasserine Pass or whatever the hell it was. So I thought, boy, the chances of getting, they didn't call anything R&R in those days, you went to war, and if the war was over you went home. So I got rid of what I had. But it was a wonderful experience.
When I retired I went out to California. I cruised all the way out there, out through Nevada, and I got nailed for driving under the influence in Nevada, and Jesus Christ, it took me a month to get out of there. Then I went down through California and Arizona. I don't drink anymore, but it used to be a part of that masculine mystique, you know. Yeah, you're, aren't you Jewish?

Aaron Elson: Yes.

Gene Crandall: We had a Jewish guy in our outfit that was a real scream. He was a corporal. And I came in the barracks one night and he was just having a damn fit, and I said to him, "What the hell's the matter with you?"
And he said, "Somebody sold one of my stores."
I said, "What the hell are you talking about?"
And he said, "I own shoe stores all the way from Maine to Florida."
And I said, "No shit." Boy, he must be a multi-millionaire. And he never said a word about anything like that. He used to get neurotic once in a while. He was just a corporal. But we had all kinds of weird guys in the service. A real interesting time, though, I'll tell you. I loved it. I never learned more in my life. And of course, when you go through an experience like that, and you watch the American will, might, conquer the world all the way from Germany to Japan and God knows every other place, you know in your mind that anything that you want to do bad enough you can do. And

you know at that time that anything in this world is possible if you are determined. But that gave me confidence all my life."

- - -

Made in the USA
Monee, IL
11 August 2021